Hummingbirds

A Beginner's Guide

Laurel Aziz

FIREFLY BOOKS

A FIREFLY BOOK

Published by Firefly Books Ltd. 2002

First Printing 2002

Publisher Cataloguing-in-Publication Data (U.S.)

Aziz, Laurel.
     Hummingbirds: a beginner's guide / Laurel Aziz.
– 1st ed.
[64] p. : col. ill. ; cm.
Includes index.
Summary: Illustrated introduction to hummingbirds.
ISBN 1-55209-487-1 (library binding)
ISBN 1-55209-372-7 (pbk.)
1. Hummingbirds – North America – Identification.
2. Bird attracting – North America I. Title.
598.7/64   21   CIP QL696.A558A95 2002

Published in the United States in 2002 by
Firefly Books (U.S.) Inc.
P.O. Box 1338, Ellicott Station
Buffalo, New York 14205

Produced by
Bookmakers Press Inc.
12 Pine Street
Kingston, Ontario K7K 1W1
(613) 549-4347
tcread@sympatico.ca

Design and layout by
Scott Nelson and Janice McLean

Printed and bound in Canada by
Friesens
Altona, Manitoba

Printed on acid-free paper

**National Library of Canada Cataloguing
in Publication Data**

Aziz, Laurel, 1956 –
     Hummingbirds : a beginner's guide

Includes index.
ISBN 1-55209-487-1 (bound)
ISBN 1-55209-372-7 (pbk.)

1. Hummingbirds – Juvenile literature. I. Title.

QL696.A558A94 2002   j598.7'64   C00-932617-0

Published in Canada in 2002 by
Firefly Books Ltd.
3680 Victoria Park Avenue
Willowdale, Ontario M2H 3K1

Front cover: Green violet-ear © Michael and Patricia Fogden
Back cover: Violet sabrewing © Michael and Patricia Fogden

The Publisher acknowledges the financial support of the Government of Canada through the Book Publishing Industry Development Program for its publishing activities.

Acknowledgments

Thanks to Bookmakers Press and to editor Tracy C. Read, art directors Scott Nelson and Janice McLean and copy editor Susan Dickinson for their inspired contributions to this project and to proofreader Catherine DeLury and indexer Mary Patton for their always impeccable work. I also want to extend my gratitude to Robert D. Montgomerie of the department of biology at Queen's University at Kingston for his careful reading and invaluable comments on the manuscript and to T. Andrew Hurly of the University of Lethbridge for the pleasure and benefit I derived from his knowledge of hummingbirds. Finally, thanks also to my publisher Lionel Koffler of Firefly Books for making this book possible.

The rufous hummingbird, a long-distance traveler, perches to feed at flowers that blossom across the Colorado landscape.

Contents

INTRODUCTION The Flower Kissers 7

PHYSICAL Small Is Beautiful 9
Built for Performance 10
Hot Little Machines 12
The Long & Short of Bills 14
The Eyes Have It 16
Glittering Fragments 18

BEHAVIOR Hummingbird Habits 23
Feasting at Flowers 24
Life on the Wing 28
Dating & Mating 30
Building a Home 32
Great Eggspectations 34
Mother Knows Best 36
Little Big Brain 40
Trip Takers 42

ECOLOGY Hummers by Nature 45
Through the Ages 46
Partners From Paradise 49
The Family Tree 52
Hazards for Hummers 54
Hummingbird Havens 56
Hummers & Humans 58

Hummers On-line 60
Photo Credits 61
Index 62

One of the widest-ranging members of the hummingbird family, the rubythroat is the only species that nests east of the Mississippi River. It is a regular inhabitant of mixed woodlands and deciduous forests and frequently visits naturalized urban spaces that have been planted with trees or bright-colored flowers.

THE FLOWER KISSERS

It had been a long, hot summer, the kind you associate with the high-pitched buzz of cicadas breaking the still air. In early spring, I had scattered the seeds for nasturtiums, hollyhocks, snapdragons and poppies in my yard, hoping that at the peak of the growing season, the orange, yellow and red blooms would be a colorful lure to transient ruby-throated hummingbirds. Now, the eye-catching flowers had come into bloom, and I waited—for weeks. I had nearly given up hope of having a hummingbird visitor in my yard when, early one morning, I heard the characteristic clicking and chirping as a tiny bird hovered at a nasturtium, flying forward and in reverse as it probed the flower for nectar. It had arrived in a flash and fed without disturbing a petal, and then it was gone.

Bird watching is one of North America's favorite outdoor pastimes, yet few members of the avian family create as much excitement as does a hummingbird when it pays a visit. Beautiful and delicate, pugnacious and tame, these fairylike birds with their rainbow-colored plumage can dive into your garden with little fanfare and instantaneously cast their magical spell. Their names evoke the splendor of their breed: berylline, brilliant, coquette, emerald, empress, magenta-throated woodstar, magnificent, mountain-gem, ruby-throated, rufous and scintillant, to name just a handful. And it is no exaggeration to suggest that with their burnished plumage and aerobatics, as they row the air in tight little figure eights, the dazzling hummingbirds are nothing short of mesmerizing.

Few of us will see more than the smallest fraction of the world's some 330 hummingbird species during our lives. Every encounter, however, treats us to the charm and mystery of the hummingbird world. In the following pages, we'll explore the hummer's intricate beauty and charm. The more you understand the nature of these birds—where they live, how they feed, nest and breed—the more rewarding you'll find the already delightful experience of meeting them face to face.

7

Perched on a twig, a wine-throated hummingbird scans the surrounding landscape. Hummers are the smallest birds in the avian world, but they more than make up for their size by being one of nature's most colorful and fascinating creatures.

Small Is Beautiful

Its iridescent plumage dazzles like gemstones as it zooms from shadow into sunlight. Its wings generate a soothing purr as they beat against the air like feathered oars. When it feeds contentedly at a red trumpet-shaped flower, staccato clicks arise like entertaining avian chat. Whether you meet one first by sight or by sound, there is no mistaking an encounter with a hummingbird.

Hummingbirds are the most distinctive of all bird families—no other is endowed with so many unique traits. The smallest species, the Cuban bee hummingbird, is the tiniest bird in the world, measuring just over two inches (5 cm) long and weighing under two grams (less than 1/10 ounce). By contrast, the largest member of the family, the giant hummingbird, is about 7½ inches (19 cm) long and weighs 20 grams (¾ ounce).

As one of the smallest of nature's warm-blooded animals, the hummingbird must work hard to survive. Like the engine of a high-performance racecar, the hummer is powerful and fast, running at an efficiently hot temperature of 105 degrees F (40°C). Its heart can pump up to a staggering 1,260 beats per minute, more than 125 times faster than the heart of the average human. Its wings, driven by powerful chest muscles, account for more than 30 percent of the hummingbird's total body weight and are the biggest (by proportion) among all birds, beating in a blur of 50 to 200 times per second. Even a hummer's slowest cruising speed—some 35 miles per hour (56 km/h)—breaks the average speed limit in most cities.

To fuel its full-burn lifestyle, a hummingbird devours half its weight in food each day without gaining an ounce! It conserves what precious excess energy its little body can store by routinely falling into a torpor each night. Not unlike your computer's "sleep" mode, this dormant state saves the hummingbird energy without completely shutting down its system.

From the tip of its saberlike bill to its tiny perching feet, the hummingbird is unusual in every way. Read on, and learn why small is, indeed, beautiful.

Built for Performance

Hummingbirds are the smallest of all birds. Most measure between 2½ and 5 inches (6-13 cm) in length and weigh from two to nine grams. A hummingbird's skeleton is light. Its hollow bones, like those of other birds, give it a pared-down skeletal structure with built-in strength and flexibility. Its modified wings enable the hummingbird to hover. The connecting arm and forearm bones from shoulder to "wrist" are reduced in size compared with those of other birds, but the hummer has elongated "hand bones," which are like our fingers but are connected end to end and run to the extreme tip of the wing skeleton. To make the oarlike motion of hovering flight possible, the hummingbird's wing sections have little flexibility, but the entire wing can be rotated at the shoulder, as we might turn our wrist.

Muscles are the flesh-and-blood machinery that converts food into energy, and the hummingbird is the muscleman among birds. The hummer's pecs are 25 to 30 per-

Hummingbirds range in length from 2½ to 7½ inches (6-19 cm). Here, a magnificent (left) and a broad-billed hummer perched on a finger provide a sense of the size of these tiny birds.

cent of its total weight, while the chest muscles of other birds are somewhere between 15 and 25 percent. Loaded with dense muscle, the hummingbird's little barrel chest is set within a sternum, or breastbone, that is proportionately the largest of all birds by depth and length.

Hummingbird muscles are built for one thing: power. Muscles move the wings up and down during flight. In most birds, the muscle that pulls the wing down is as much as 10 times larger than the one that raises the wing. In the hummer, however, it is only twice as big. The relative similarity in muscle size reveals the importance of both the upstroke and the downstroke for hovering flight.

The main energy source of muscles is mitochondria, the storage site for chemicals that allow muscles to do their work. To increase the efficiency of their output, hummingbird muscles contain 35 percent mitochondria, nearly double the content of most mammalian muscles. (The cheetah's sudden bursts of incredible speed are likewise fueled by mitochondria.) The mitochondria-rich, ultraefficient design of hummingbird muscles saves on space and energy. Without this so-called double-packing, a hummer's muscles would need to be much larger and bulkier to produce the same energy, and they would cease to be an efficient

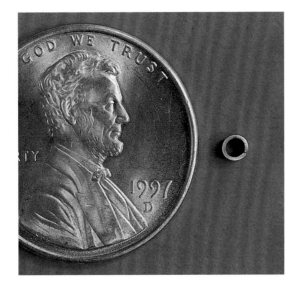

A fraction of the size of a penny, a hummingbird leg band, above, used by researchers to track birds, must be small enough to stay on the magnificent hummer's tiny "ankle," below, without slipping off.

design for helicopter-style flight.

The hummingbird's lifestyle has reduced the importance of its feet. With the exception of a few high-altitude tropical species that peck insects from the ground—the Andean hillstar, bearded helmetcrest and thornbills, for instance—the vast majority of hummingbird species have tiny feet. Although small, they're handy for perching, which is how the hummer spends some 80 percent of its day, and dexterous for wiping its bill, preening and scratching feathers. In flight, the feet are positioned like the landing gear of an airplane, tucked tight against its belly.

Hummingbirds delight us with their antics and their beauty. Through millions of years of adaptation, they have become specialist creatures, just another reminder that these tiny jewels on the wing are more than a colorful adornment on the natural landscape.

Hot Little Machines

It takes a lot of energy to be a hummingbird. That energy is created through a chemical process called metabolism, by which the body converts food into fuel for a variety of activities necessary for survival.

Warm-blooded animals must maintain a stable body temperature even when there are temperature fluctuations in the environment. The hummingbird pushes the edge of the metabolic envelope. When active, its normal body temperature is close to 105 degrees F (40°C). The hummer's heart, which, for its size, is proportionately the largest among all birds, also beats the fastest,

The heart rate of a blue-throated hummingbird has been measured at a record-breaking 1,260 beats per minute; the hummer's average rate is a less speedy 650 beats per minute.

registering an average 650 beats per minute. The blue-throated hummingbird's ticker has been clocked at an incredible 1,260 beats per minute. This hardworking muscle circulates blood that carries more oxygen than the hearts of other birds and is also more efficient at unloading oxygen into the tissues that need it. Even when a hummer is at rest, its metabolism is at least four times higher than that of a pigeon.

It is vital that a warm-blooded animal doesn't lose more energy than it generates. The smaller the animal, the faster its metabolic rate and the faster it loses heat to the environment. Because of the hummingbird's size, there is little margin for error, and each day is a delicate balancing act between life and death. In fact, the tiniest hummer—the two-gram Cuban bee hummingbird—represents the lowest critical size for survival of any warm-blooded vertebrate. It is matched in size only by the equally lightweight Etruscan shrew and the Thai bumblebee bat. Conserving heat is one way that warm-blooded animals regulate their body temperature. For birds, fat and feathers provide insulation that can trap and hold body heat. An additional strategy used by hummers to cope with heat loss is known as torpor. When temperatures are cool or when food is scarce, certain hummingbird species are able to slow down all bodily functions, effectively lowering their body temperature

A hovering broad-tailed hummingbird keeps its strength up by foraging for high-energy nectar.

so that they can stay alive at a low rate of energy expenditure. It is estimated that their metabolism drops to one-fiftieth its normal rate. Torpor also decreases the rate of water loss.

Since the hummingbird possesses a minimum amount of body fat to store excess fuel, it has solved its metabolic challenges through diet. Its choice of nectar—the highest energy food available—is one of the keys to the hummingbird's success, and a healthy part of a hummer's day is spent in search of food. A special gut rapidly moves sugar into the hummer's system to produce energy to fuel its body. Even with its power diet, a hummingbird consumes half its weight in sugar every day. According to one researcher, it would take the nectar production of more than 1,000 fuchsia blossoms to sustain a male Anna's hummingbird each day. If a full-grown man were to burn energy at the same rate, he would have to consume 155,000 calories per day—the equivalent of close to 250 Big Macs—to survive.

The hummingbird exists on a threshold of critical extremes, but it has no alternative. If it were any bigger, it would be unable to maintain hovering flight; any smaller, and there wouldn't be enough hours in the day to eat what would be necessary to ensure its survival. The demanding energy output of the hummer's lifestyle is an example of nature's precision in shaping and molding a species.

The Long & Short of Bills

In spring, it is a lance wielded by rival hummingbirds jousting for control of a territory. In summer, it is a knitting needle used to gather and stitch downy plant fibers into the walls of a snug little nest. Hundreds of times each day, it is used as a probe into the well of nectar hidden at the base of a blossom. The elongated bill of a hummingbird is, without a doubt, one of its most distinctive and functional features, serving as both hands and mouth.

A hummingbird bill consists of a horn-like material whose primary structural protein is keratin. A hardened version of the epidermis, or outer layer of skin, keratin is also found in hooves, skin, feathers and human fingernails. Generally speaking, a hummingbird bill is disproportionately longer than the bird's head (and sometimes its body) and extends to a needlelike point. When closed, the bill is circular in cross section, rather than bent like the bill of the flamingo or spatulate like the bill of the spoonbill. While some exotic hummers have red bills, such as the violet-crowned, the buff-bellied, the white-eared and the berylline hummers, most are black or dark brown.

There is tremendous variation in the length and shape of hummingbird bills. The shortest bill—less than ½ inch (1.3 cm) —is owned by the purple-backed thornbill. The longest bill belongs to the appropriately named sword-billed hummingbird, whose four-inch (10 cm) bill almost matches its body length. Bills range from straight to downcurved (in most tropical species) to slightly upturned at the end,

Hummingbird bills come in all shapes and sizes and often match the contours of the flowers at which these birds feed. The elongated bill of the green-fronted lancebill, top, is well suited to deep tubular flowers, while the bearded helmetcrest's short, straight bill, above, is a better fit for flowers with an open face.

14

with a few that are dramatically shaped like scythes or sickles.

While there isn't always an exact connection between bill and flower length, a hummingbird bill is the direct result of the hummer's lifestyle as a nectar-feeder and often matches the size and shape of many of the hummer's favorite flowers. The more ordinary the bill, the greater the variety of flowers at which the bird can feed. The more specialized the bill, however, the more exclusive the relationship between bird and flower. The sword-billed hummingbird, for example, has a monopoly on feeding at certain passionflowers whose extremely deep blossoms harbor nectar reserves that are beyond the reach of any less specialized bill. Wherever there is a specialized hum-

The bills of the white-tipped sicklebill, above, and the violet sabrewing, below, fit perfectly into the hard-to-reach flowers of the heliconia.

mingbird bill, there is a tongue to match. The hummingbird laps up nectar with its tongue. Each hummer's tongue is basically as long as its bill, and the hyoid bone at the base of the tongue allows the bird to extend its tongue beyond the bill tip. Divided into separate sections, or lobes, in the front half, the tongue is fringed on the outer edges and ridged around the perimeter. It is believed that when the hummer feeds, it curls the fringed outer edges of each lobe inward, forming a pair of tubes. When feeding, the hummer rapidly inserts and removes its tongue at the rate of 13 times per second, while capillary action draws nectar into its mouth.

The best time to watch a hummingbird is when it is poised at a feeder. Notice how it flies forward to a flower and inserts its bill, its darting tongue extracting nectar. As it pulls back from the feeder, study the shape and contour of its bill, one of the most telling aspects of hummingbird design.

The Eyes Have It

A hummingbird appears out of nowhere and makes a beeline to the nearest flower. Arriving at its target, it screeches to a halt in midair, its tail end swinging like a pendulum from the sudden stop. But before you can point and say its name, the hummingbird has sped away.

All birds rely heavily on vision to survive: to find food sources, to avoid predators and to participate in social behaviors like nest building and caring for their young. Good vision is especially important to precision fliers like hummingbirds.

A bird's eyes occupy a proportionately large volume of its head. Positioned high and near the sides of its head, a hummingbird's eyes give it a glimpse of attackers approaching from above. Each of the hummer's eyes measures six to eight millimeters in diameter, and both are firmly locked in their sockets, which forces the bird to move its head when it needs to see a wider field. Because the hummingbird hawks, or captures, insects in flight, it needs sharp vision. Its eyes are globular, like those of eagles and other birds of prey. When a hummer looks to the side, it has monocular vision (it sees with one eye only); when it looks straight

Research shows that hummers are not innately drawn just to red flowers. Flowers that blossom in bright colors, like monarda, left, stand out in the temperate landscape. In the green tropical understory, below, they attract birds like the white-vented violet-ear, opposite.

forward, its vision is binocular. It also has what is known as a nictitating membrane, a transparent third eyelid under the lower lid that closes over the eyeball to moisten or protect it during flight.

The light-sensitive membrane of the eyeball that transmits images to the brain is called the retina. The internal structure of the retina is made up of rods and cones, cells that contain light-sensitive pigments. The rods function in low light and are abundant in the eyes of night-active birds such as owls. Although highly sensitive to light, these cells provide poor perception. Cones, on the other hand, allow birds to see shapes and colors. The eyes of birds that hunt for stationary objects must differentiate fine detail and are therefore loaded with cones.

Fast-flying birds like the hummingbird must be able to adjust their focus quickly. The fovea centralis at the back of the eye is rich in cones and may be an important region of the hummingbird's retina for detecting details in the lush landscape. The hummer uses the fovea centralis when it is looking to the left or to the right and moves its head to bring an object into focus.

For members of the hummingbird family, color is an important part of social life as well as basic survival. Insects don't see color, while birds do. Hummingbirds are one of the rare noninsect species that live largely on nectar, so a colorful blossom is a flower's way of saying it would rather attract hummers than other pollinator species like insects. Researchers suggest that red has, almost by default, become a signal between flowers and the hummingbirds they attract.

Many experiments have been conducted to determine whether hummingbirds actually have a preference for red, but in fact, they don't. They do, however, associate color with food sources, and researchers speculate that the color stands out like a flag in the hummingbirds' world. In the overwhelming green of their tropical environment, red —the color complement of green—is a beacon against the background vegetation.

The social life of many hummingbird species is also influenced by color. While hummingbirds themselves are colorful birds, the color red shows up only sparingly in their plumage. Appearing on their gorgets (throat patches) and head crests, it can be hidden or revealed at will and flashed as a badge of authority to communicate a range of messages, from aggression to flirtation.

Glittering Fragments

The feature that distinguishes birds from all other creatures is feathers, and they have achieved no more harmonious marriage of form and function than in the hummingbird's plumage.

Feathers are an amazing bit of natural engineering that allows birds to fly. Aerodynamically sound, they are capable of loft for flight, offer good insulation and are precious to overall health. The hollow feather shaft, called the rachis, is composed of keratin—the hornlike material found in our fingernails and in the covering of a bird's bill—which makes a sturdy but light backbone for supporting the feather struc-

A violet-headed hummingbird uses its bill to groom and clean its feathers, below. A hovering long-tailed sylph, opposite, displays its spectacular green tail plumes.

ture. The quill is lined with barbs, individual filaments that knit or hook together in a weblike fashion, making the feather waterproof, windproof and resilient. Fluffy barbs on the lower part of the quill add to the feather's insulating ability.

Hummingbird feathers are extraordinary. The body feathers are short and very tightly packed together—"as close as fishes' scales" is how one historic writer described them. For its body size, a hummingbird has a feather density five times greater than that of a thrush. Extremely long primary and secondary flight feathers give the wings an oversized appearance.

The magnificent color of its feathers, however, makes the hummingbird one of the most beautiful wild creatures to watch. American painter and ornithologist John James Audubon reported that his encounter with a ruby-throated hummingbird was like seeing a "glittering fragment of the rainbow," while one native American name for hummingbirds translates into "beams or locks of the Sun."

Among hummingbird species, the hermits, which are tropical, tend to be duller, with the male and female similarly colored. By contrast, non-hermits generally have more brilliant colors in their plumage and display considerable variation between males and females.

The secret to this richly colored plumage is its iridescence, which is known as a structural color. Whereas the feather colors of some birds are pro-

duced by a variety of pigments, humming-bird feathers contain only two melanin pigments that produce black and red tones, such as those found in the plumage of the rufous hummingbird. With a few exceptions, hummingbird feathers derive their iridescence from microscopic platelets, or air bubbles, in the barbules on the top third of the feather. Factors such as the size and thickness of these air sacs, the amount of available light and the angle at which light hits the surface of the feather all play a part in determining the colors we see in the plumage. (That's why scientists sometimes refer to iridescence as interference coloration.) Depending on the angle of light striking the plumage, the human eye can see some or all of an array of colors along the spectrum, from red to green

An important asset for all birds, feathers require constant care. Besides combing and grooming their feathers, hummingbirds frequently bathe by darting through garden sprinklers, splashing in puddles or dipping in water-filled leaves.

to violet and blue. In shadow, a humming-bird might appear as a solid, shiny dark color or even black. Yet in sunlight, the plumage is an ever-shifting kaleidoscope of shimmering metallic emerald greens and sapphire blues.

Feathers serve a social function as well, playing a role in communication. Some feathers on the outer ends of the wings are designed to produce sound like the signature hummingbird "hum." Among non-hermit hummers, there is a tremendous difference in plumage between males and females. Males sport colorful throat patches, or gorgets, and head crests. The most grandiose feathers, however, occur in elaborate tail adornments that can be forked, scissorlike, wedge-shaped, round or pointed. These feather flourishes are used among the birds like flash cards, selectively shown and dramatically raised and ruffled to intimidate or attract other birds.

The care and regeneration of hummingbird feathers are a lifelong responsibility and an energetically taxing process. Like all birds, the hummer spends a lot of time taking care of its feathers, as they are among the little bird's most precious assets. Feathers require constant cleaning and preening to keep pests under control, and the hummingbird can often be seen perched on a leaf that holds rainwater, bathing itself. It can also flick water onto its plumage and comb it through with its bill or ruffle and groom the feathers with its claws.

The hummingbird molts before it is a year old, then annually after

A rufous hummingbird's shimmering gorget, above, and the iridescent plumage of a green-crowned brilliant, below, are the result of light dancing across the feather surfaces.

that. The molt takes seven to eight months in total as the wing feathers fall out and regrow sequentially, starting with the first primary. Between 20 and 40 percent of the bird's energy is expended shedding and regrowing feathers. The bird is still able to fly during that time, but the tattered feathers compromise the plumage's overall water resistance and insulation value, as well as the bird's aerial maneuverability. Some research suggests that the hummingbird does what it can to maintain the status quo. By expending more energy, one molting female rubythroat was able to compensate for as much as a 30 percent loss in the surface area of her wings.

Throughout the ages, the diminutive hummingbird has been admired for its beauty, and its feathers have been prized as fashion adornments from the time of the Aztecs to the Victorian era. As our knowledge of hummingbird biology grows through observation and study, we continue to respond to the inherent beauty of these flying jewels.

With its tail fanned for stability, a scintillant hummingbird makes an acrobatic approach to a flowering heath. The 2½-inch-long (6 cm) bird regularly poaches nectar from the territories of larger species.

Hummingbird Habits

Why do territorial hummingbirds defend their food sources? Why, in contrast, do hermits fly through the tropical-forest understory feeding at undefended patches of flowers, like fur trappers collecting pelts? What is the importance of memory in a hummingbird's life? How and why is hummingbird flight different from that of other birds?

Historically, the scientists who first studied hummingbirds had their hands full simply reporting the variety of behaviors they witnessed, such as flight, feeding, courtship, nest building and parenting. Later, however, scientists working with the benefit of the theory of evolution were able to show that animal behaviors, from the ordinary to the unusual, are more than whimsical actions. Although these behaviors may be puzzling to humans, they serve a purpose and have endured, or been "selected," because they increase an animal's success in its environment.

Why study behavior? One reason is purely recreational: A hummingbird is fascinating to watch. In addition to its sheer physical beauty, this tiny creature delights us with its antics. But by observing the hummingbird and posing questions, we will discover interesting facts about its life that will enrich our experience.

Such understanding can be much more than an idle pastime. Humans are unique among animals. Only we have the power, through our actions, to disrupt natural ecosystems and displace and destroy native species. Yet when we understand the function of particular behaviors in the hummingbird's life—that it uses spider silk to anchor its nest, that the rufous hummingbird feeds on the sequentially blooming candlestick flowers as it migrates through the southwestern desert each year, that tropical species meet at ancestral mating sites, that the hummer, or its offspring, has bull's-eye accuracy in returning to its familiar nesting site for years on end—we are gathering vital knowledge that can be used to protect the hummingbird, its environment and the species on which it depends.

Feasting at Flowers

Hummingbird life revolves around food. Because of its small size and high energy output, the hummingbird has a voracious appetite. It is estimated that a hummingbird typically consumes half its weight in sugar each day. (One scientist observed that during an active day, a hummingbird made 15 feeding trips per hour, visiting many flowers on each trip.) Its chosen source of fuel is high-energy nectar, which most species drink from flowers. But a handful of migratory hummingbirds also lap up sap from tree trunks that have been bored by sapsuckers and woodpeckers.

The abundance and diversity of flowering plants explain much about the widespread success of the hummingbird family. Nectar is readily available in a variety of habitats, from humid tropical rainforests and temperate forests to arid deserts and high alpine zones. The hummingbird family occupies all these areas.

The hummingbird feeding strategy is about more than a random sweet tooth. Laboratory studies have found that the

Nectar takes the fast track through the digestive system of this magenta-throated woodstar.

hummingbird discriminates between flower types on the basis of nectar quality, concentration and rate of flow. It chooses nectar with between 20 and 25 percent sugar concentration, and these studies verify that sugar concentration is more important than the color of the flower in determining which blossoms a hummingbird will visit.

Using their lancelike bills, two Anna's hummingbirds joust for territorial control.

The diversity of flowering plants and habitats has also encouraged a variety of feeding strategies within the hummingbird family. Two common strategies identify a hummingbird as either a territorialist or a trapliner.

Like a property owner, a territorialist works hard to defend the patch of flowers where it harvests nectar. The area must be large enough to provide adequate food but small enough to be easily defended. A territorialist spends a lot of time confronting trespassing hummers by dive-bombing, chattering angrily and raising its feather crest and gorget in an effort to intimidate intruders and prevent them from feeding. Some of the best-known territorialists tend to be medium-sized hummingbirds capable of great flight acceleration, such as emeralds, sunangels and pufflegs.

Depending on the nectar flow, a hummingbird's territory can range from a densely packed larder no more than a dozen feet across to a larger site that boasts thousands of blossoms. The goal for the bird is to maximize the reward and to min-

A Complete Diet

Although nectar is a high-energy food, it lacks many nutrients. Hummingbirds supplement their diet with insects and spiders, which provide protein, minerals, fat and vitamins and are digested much more slowly. While the ratio of insect meals to nectar meals differs with each species, scientists estimate that hummingbirds spend one-quarter of their foraging time hunting for insects and the rest of it feeding at flowers.

Hummingbirds use two methods for capturing insects. In the first, known as hawking, the hummingbird grabs an insect while in flight; this behavior is common to hummingbirds with straight bills, such as the rubythroat, whether they are nabbing their insect meals on the wing or near the ground. Species with curved bills, like the hermits, "glean" insects from spiderwebs and the edges of plant leaves. Their bills are slightly less maneuverable and therefore not as suited to snatching a moving target.

Flower Power

In contrast to territorial hummingbirds, which typically defend a single-species flower patch, trapliners frequently feed at many flower species as they travel through the forest. From the plant's point of view, the one drawback to such door-to-door visits from generalist hummingbird feeders is that pollen may be transported to plants other than its own species, which means some plants will fail to reproduce.

To help defend against their pollen

Here, pollen is carried between flowers on the bill of the purple-throated mountain-gem.

being wasted, trap-lined flowers have evolved so that their stamens—the pollen-bearing male parts of the flower—are uniquely positioned within the blossom. When a hummer visits a passionflower, for instance, pollen brushes against its forehead and crown; its throat may already be covered with pollen from another flower species. Continuing on its way, the hummer will relay passionflower pollen only to other passionflowers, when its forehead comes in contact with the female pistil.

imize the area that needs to be defended—in other words, to get the greatest amount of food for the least amount of effort. Researchers have shown that a hummer will adjust the size of a territory to add or lose flowers according to its needs.

The hummingbird will defend a territory against rivals of its own species and of the opposite sex and even against insects and other bird species. The highly territorial rufous hummingbird works hard to protect its food sources, giving chase to an intruder that crosses the line of its territory. While dramatic feather displays or head waving is often used to threaten a rival, the Anna's hummingbird makes an aggressive and direct assault on an intruder when there is a lot of food at stake. In such confron-

tations, a hummingbird uses its bill as a lance to attack the intruder.

A trapliner, on the other hand, like the fur trappers from whom the name is derived, feeds at a number of flowers spread over familiar, well-traveled routes. While these hummers don't defend patches of flowers, trapliner species, such as the hermit hummingbirds that live in the Costa Rican rainforests, tend to visit flowers particularly suited to their bill shape. The hermits, for example, with their long, down-curved bill, favor deep tubular flowers like the heliconia, while the sicklebills, which have a scythelike bill, are frequent visitors to flowers like the lobelia.

Traplining hummingbirds themselves are divided into two broad groups, known as high-reward and low-reward trapliners. High-reward trapliners, like the hermits, are choosy feeders that select flowers offering a good and reliable supply of nectar. An example of a generalist low-reward trapliner is the female purple-throated mountain-gem, which, conversely, is a generalist feeder that opportunistically visits a variety of far-flung flowers.

Hummingbirds don't always fall neatly into these foraging categories, however. Many simply sneak past or blatantly raid the flower patches of territorialists. Marauders, which tend to be among the larger hummers, use their heft to help themselves

The long-tailed hermit pollinates and feeds at the heliconia's flower bract, whose elongated shape excludes generalist insect pollinators.

to food in another bird's territory. Filchers, on the other hand, follow the path of least resistance, sneaking their food from an established territory when the territory owner heads off in pursuit of another intruder. One ingenious variation on the filcher's way of life is demonstrated by the magenta-throated woodstar, famous for its beelike buzzing. The imitative behavior is so convincing that the woodstar can enter a territory and feed at a flower in full view of its permanent resident. Similarly, the smooth, quiet mothlike flight of the black-crested coquette enables it to poach a meal from the territory of other hummingbirds.

There are as many feeding styles and preferences as there are hummingbird species. Each one has devised a solution to surviving in a highly competitive world. ⅄

Life on the Wing

In their ability to fly, birds are unusual among all vertebrates, with the exception of bats. The hummingbird, however, can do better—it flies forward, backward, up, down and sideways, which makes it the only bird with the maneuverability of a helicopter.

All flight is a battle against gravity and friction. The force that lifts a bird into the air (and prevents it from falling) is called lift, and it is created by airflow over and around the wings. When air moves faster over the top of the wing than under it, a bird is buoyed into the air.

For most birds, then, the powerful flight stroke occurs when the wings beat down, while the upward stroke is a recovery stroke that finishes the cycle. For the hummingbird, though, the two strokes are equal in power. It is the hummingbird's ability to generate power during the upstroke as well as the downstroke that enables it to hover.

The hummingbird is the Hercules of the bird world. The muscles that power its upstroke are strong. The upstroke muscles

In flight, a hummingbird keeps its tiny feet tucked tight against its belly. This scintillant extends its feet as it comes in for a landing.

weigh almost half as much as the downstroke muscles, which is nearly 10 times their proportional weight in other birds. Overall, the hummingbird boasts unusually large chest muscles. Compared with the chest muscles of most birds and humans, which occupy roughly 20 percent and 5 percent, respectively, of their total body mass, a hummingbird's chest muscles represent as much as 30 percent of its total body weight and are the reason for its strength in flight.

Its skeletal adaptations also assist in hovering flight. The hummingbird has relatively long wings in proportion to its body size. To generate the power needed for flight, the wings are very mobile and can turn 180 degrees, or completely over, at the "wrist" to create the powerful upstroke. The hummingbird's deeply keeled sternum and eight ribs, rather than six (as with other birds), help fortify the skeleton when the bird is vigorously pumping its wings.

The movement of the hummingbird's wings has long been a source of fascination. Before leaving its perch, a hummingbird begins its flight with a series of split-second strokes that help it achieve nearly its top speed and maintain control from the launch. In forward flight, the hummingbird uses a form of flapping flight, with its wings beating in an oval pattern against the air. By tilting the angle, or plane, of the wings, the hummer can make a variety of directional maneuvers—up, down, forward and backward. When it hovers, however, a hummingbird traces a figure eight in the air, with its wings parallel to the ground.

Whereas many birds conserve energy by gliding or soaring, the hummingbird has become a precision flier that specializes in hovering, which is the most strenuous form of flight. Its wing beats vary from 15 beats per second in the giant hummingbird to a staggering 80 beats per second in the amethyst woodstar.

The hummingbird is the most aerobically active warm-blooded animal on Earth, and its feats of prolonged hovering are achieved by no other creature. Although flight is energetically expensive, it is the defining trait of the hummingbird's existence. Much more than a way to get around, flight is fundamental to the family's specialized behaviors—from territorial defense, courtship and mating to feeding and nest building—and to its ultimate success.

In hovering flight, a male snowcap, above, and a female rufous hummingbird, below, "row" the air in perpetual figure eights.

Dating & Mating

In the hummingbird's social life, there is sometimes a fine line between love and hate. Many of the courtship behaviors displayed by the male hummingbird when trying to attract a mate, for instance, closely resemble the aggressive actions he uses when defending a patch of flowers.

Courtship is one of the most elaborate social behaviors among birds. North Ameri-

Like a king dressed in elaborate ceremonial garments, the male tufted coquette flares his arresting head crest and glimmering throat patch in anticipation of entering the dating game.

can hummingbirds breed during the spring and summer, in concert with the warm weather, an abundant supply of nectar and the explosion of insect populations.

Some biologists divide courtship into two parts. The first is luring, or attracting, the female; the second is the mating phase. During the first phase, the male hummingbird employs song, plumage displays and acrobatic flight to attract a mate. Visual displays are common among courting male North American hummingbird species. While these may vary with the species, many male hummers engage in a variety of aerobatics, presenting their glittering plumage or flared gorgets and featuring postures and behavior that reveal colorful feathers or include vocalizations or sounds made with the feathers.

One of the best-known aerial displays is that of the Anna's hummingbird. During courtship, the male flies to heights of anywhere from 75 to 150 feet (23-46 m) while looking down at the female. The male then swoops down over the female's head and emits a loud popping sound, which is generated by the male's tail feathers.

Another courtship display, called the shuttle flight, is used by the Anna's, the ruby-throated, the rufous, the Allen's, the Costa's and the calliope. In this demonstration, the male makes a short-distance, back-and-forth flight within a foot of the perching female. These "shuttle flights" are done singly or in a series of up to eight repeated patterns, and they are often performed in the center of the male's territory. To accompany the display, some species produce a sound by rustling their feathers, while others make a "buzzing" vocalization.

The ruby-throated hummingbird's courtship flight, on the other hand, is like a clock pendulum that swings in a wide methodical arc. When the male brushes close to the head of the observing female, he makes a buzzing sound. There are variations on this courtship theme, however, that have the male and female facing each other and bobbing up and down a few feet in the air, like alternating pistons. These displays are riveting for a female.

Many hummingbird species also gather together in leks. Such gatherings contain anywhere from a few to a hundred male participants. Only a handful of North American hummingbird species—the blue-throated, the white-eared and the berylline—form these groups. The resulting all-male choir attracts females looking for a partner. Some of the meeting sites for leks are ancestral and have been used for more than a dozen years, with up to 25 male birds participating each time.

Tropical species, such as the little hermit, the green hermit and the long-tailed hermit, are more likely to participate in leks. These birds are not as brilliantly colored, and their habitat, which is typically closed forest canopy, is dark. Elaborate vocalization by the male birds may be one of the best ways to attract the attention of the females that visit

A female rubythroat, above, perches to appreciate the display of a courting male flying overhead. With its gorget flared, a male calliope hummingbird, below, sails past a female, flamboyantly signaling for her attention.

these sites for the sole purpose of mating.

By whatever social ritual the male and female forge a bond, the connection is brief, lasting only as long as it takes them to mate. With hummingbirds, as with many bird families, all the responsibility for nesting and caring for the young falls to the female. After building a nest, the female seeks out a mate, and shortly after mating, she is on her own to tend the nest and raise her offspring.

Building a Home

The hummingbird's meticulously designed and constructed nest is first and foremost a place to lay eggs, but it also provides the hummer with a warm place to sleep at night and a safe, sheltered haven for raising its young. The female hummingbird is the family architect, taking anywhere from two days to two weeks to complete the struc-

The Anna's hummingbird, below, has built its cup-shaped nest on a pinecone, while the straight-billed hermit, right, has fashioned a pendulous nest on the tip of a rainforest leaf.

ture. Like all wild creatures, the hummingbird adapts its nest to suit the surroundings, using the materials at hand—plant stems, twigs, moss, lichens and plant down.

The most common style—constructed by hummingbird species such as the ruby-throated, Anna's, black-chinned and rufous—is an open cup-shaped nest that can house two eggs and the mother bird. The pendulous nest, common among resident tropical species, is a tapered, conelike structure attached to a broad, blade-shaped leaf that forms the inner wall.

The nests of different hummingbird species are variations on a theme: compact, insulated, camouflaged little incubators for the hummers' eggs. The hummingbird is hot-blooded and maintains a body temperature of 105 degrees F (40°C). With a demanding metabolism that burns food at a high rate and a small body mass to store excess energy, a hummingbird must protect itself against the chilling effects of cool temperatures, whether it inhabits the tropics or temperate zones. A well-built nest offers protection against the elements and preserves the body heat necessary to incubate the tiny eggs.

The rubythroat is one of only five hummingbird species that breed in Canada and is one of the most widely distributed hummingbirds in the New World. Each year, in a Herculean display of strength, it flies over

600 miles (960 km) of open water, across the Gulf of Mexico, en route from its winter home in Central America to its summer breeding grounds in the North. To solve the potentially life-threatening problem of heat loss during cool northern nights, the hummingbird pads the walls of its eggcup-sized nest with a thick layer of fluffy down gathered from plants such as milkweed and dandelion.

Hummingbirds are the smallest birds in the world and, accordingly, build the smallest and most vulnerable nests. The nests of most North American species are one inch (2.5 cm) deep and have less than two inches (5 cm) between the inside walls. To improve the structural integrity of these pint-sized homes, each species uses spider silk—the strongest material in nature—to bind the nest together and to anchor it to the tree-branch foundation. This con-

A slender branch provides adequate support for the black-chinned hummingbird's nest.

struction innovation reveals something about the hummer's unequaled speed, its helicopter-style maneuverability and the dexterity of its specialized bill, which is perfectly suited to manipulating the impossibly sticky micron-diameter filaments of silk.

The most striking feature of any hummingbird's nest is its camouflage. The hummer positions and designs its nest to blend into the surrounding landscape. When the

basic structure of the nest is complete, the exterior is decorated with colorful fragments of lichen and moss that not only add to its beauty but render it invisible amid the vegetation where it is placed.

While all hummingbird species share the same basic design concepts, they vary widely in where they like to locate their nests. The bronzy metallic calliope hummingbird that breeds in mountainous areas from California to British Columbia makes a habit of building its nest atop a cluster of cones in a coniferous tree, much as historic barns and farmhouses stand on fieldstone foundations. The white-eared hummingbird wedges its nest in the crotch of a tree, thoroughly lashing the nesting materials to the stable branches. In tropical Costa Rica, the long-tailed hermit constructs a pendulous nest on the underside of a broad palm or banana leaf, literally putting a roof over its head. The cocoon of plant fibers, which looks like a sleeping bag made of toasted shredded coconut, is thereby protected from heavy tropical rains.

By looking at its nest, you can learn a lot about a hummingbird. Despite the hummer's delicate jewel-like appearance, the tenacious little bird has devised innovative construction solutions to the many challenges shared by all living creatures trying to build a home.

Great Eggspectations

A great feat of bioengineering, a bird's egg is a self-contained microenvironment that protects and nourishes a developing embryo. The hard exterior shell is made of calcium carbonate, the same material present in seashells. This brittle exterior, however, is lined with a rubbery membrane that seals in the liquid albumen (which bathes the developing embryo) and the yolk (which is the embryo's high-protein food). All the while, this unique shell construction allows for the exchange of oxygen with the outside environment.

For birds in general, it is physically taxing to lay these amniotic eggs. For hummingbirds, eggs demand a lot of energy. Most bird eggs represent less than 5 percent of the female's weight. Consider the ostrich, which lays the largest egg among birds. Even at 6½ inches (16.5 cm) long and weighing a little more than three pounds (1.5 kg), this giant among bird eggs represents less than 2 percent of the ostrich's total weight. By contrast, the largest hummingbird egg, which is laid by the giant hummer, is no bigger than an oversized jelly bean. But even though more than 1,000 of those tiny eggs would fit

Ostrich, chicken and hummingbird eggs (from left to right) indicate the dramatic diversity among birds and their eggs.

inside an ostrich egg, each one accounts for anywhere between 10 and 20 percent of the hummer's total body weight. So it is a strenuous exercise for the hummer to produce the two eggs per clutch that a female typically lays over a two-day stretch.

After they are laid in the nest, hummingbird eggs, like all bird eggs, require almost constant care. The mother is the little avian incubator, generating the heat to keep the eggs at a steady 93 degrees F (33.8°C). The source of warmth is the brood patch, an area on the incubating bird's chest that is rich with blood vessels. The oblong shape of the eggs exposes the maximum area for incubation. To make sure she is warming the eggs consistently, the female turns them with her bill. In the early days of incubation, the female spends anywhere from 60 to 80 percent of the day on her nest, leaving only for short trips to feed herself.

It takes from 15 to 22 days for hummingbird eggs to become hummingbird hatchlings. The Andean hillstar has the longest incubation period among all hummingbirds, lasting about 22 days. When the developing embryo has grown to the stage that it has used up its food supply within the shell, the hummingbird chick is ready to emerge. Before it hatches, the chick develops two temporary features that help it break out of the shell. The first, an egg tooth, is a bony tip on its bill; the other is a strong muscle on the back of the chick's head. The muscle gives the chick the strength to drive the egg tooth through the shell and thereby enter the world.

A newly hatched black-chinned hummingbird, right, struggles free of its shell, while a female crowned woodnymph, below, diligently incubates eggs in her tiny lichen-covered cup nest.

35

Mother Knows Best

Incubating the eggs and raising the chicks are exclusively the female hummingbird's responsibility. Even before the female mates, her life as a single mother begins when she chooses a site near a reliable food source to build her nest. The strategic location eases the job of feeding herself and the two broods of chicks she may raise each year.

Nesting is one of the most intensive

In anticipation of leaving the nest, two broad-tailed fledglings, below, test their wings. A stripe-tailed female, opposite, feeds a chick.

times of maternal care. To maintain the warmth of the eggs and the young chicks, the female must be on the nest almost constantly. One scientist set out to determine how much work it takes to raise a brood of hummingbirds. In studying three species —the broad-billed, the violet-crowned and the black-chinned hummingbirds, which nest in southeastern Arizona and southwestern New Mexico—he found that the female hummer spends nearly 60 percent of her time constructing the nest versus being away from it. Once the eggs are laid, the female spends up to 85 percent of her time on the nest incubating. On half of the occasions when the mother leaves the nest, it is only because she has been disturbed or forced to defend it.

Hummingbird chicks hatch in what is known as an "altricial" state. Helpless, naked and blind, they rely completely on the mother for warmth and food. During nesting, the female does not use torpor to conserve energy. Instead, she is on full throttle for up to two weeks, trying to maintain a cozy environment for her offspring. In one study, the interior of a well-insulated Anna's hummingbird nest registered about 50 Fahrenheit degrees (28 Celsius degrees) warmer than the external air temperature. Within two weeks, the offspring have the ability to keep themselves warm throughout the night.

Even before their eyes open, the nestlings instinctively open their tiny bills to beg for food. The mother energetically pumps regurgitated nectar and insects

Teamwork

The male hummingbird has virtually no involvement in family life. More than 50 years ago, observers reported two separate incidents of male violet-ears incubating eggs, and there is the occasional sighting of males feeding the young. But some researchers think these are simply cases of mistaken identity between the sexes.

There are reports, however, of male hummingbirds provisioning, or bringing food to, the female as she incubates the eggs. Occasionally, these records mention northern species, such as the ruby-throated, Anna's and rufous hummingbirds, which suggests that northerly species benefit from a team effort.

In 1991, scientists in Costa Rica observed an adult band-tailed barbthroat delivering food to another adult incubating eggs. They recorded more than 200 occasions when the nonincubating bird approached the nest.

In one-third of these visits, the birds touched bills, which led the researchers to conclude that the visiting bird was feeding the nesting bird. Although the scientists were unable to determine the sex of the visiting bird, they considered the possibility that it was a female which had lost her own brood and, in an imitative behavior, was provisioning another incubating female.

A hot-blooded incubator, the rufous-tailed hummingbird, hunched down in her nest, keeps her eggs warm until they hatch.

down their throats one to three times each hour. But she is engaged in a balancing act of caring for her young and taking a minimum number of breaks to feed and provision herself. When it comes to nurturing dependent offspring, afternoon attention is the most intense, and the female uses evenings to feed heartily before settling in for the night.

The female hummingbird typically produces a small clutch of two eggs, which makes it possible for her to work alone. By doing so, she helps keep the location of the nest secret, thereby increasing the security of the hummingbird family.

When it comes to protecting her young, the female is aggressive. Small as she is, the female hummer has been seen attacking all kinds of predators, from nest-robbing jays to snakes and carnivorous insects. Despite the female's attentive nature, the hummingbird still experiences a poor level of nestling success, as the chicks are vulnerable to a host of threats, including predation and bad weather. The most accomplished of the hummers in raising chicks to maturity is the Andean hillstar, which has a 60 percent success rate.

Hummingbird chicks develop quickly from pinfeathers to contour feathers, skipping over the downy stage common to many songbird species. Young hummers start preening and caring for their feathers at about 16 days. Most chicks are ready to fly after 21 days, even though the mother continues to feed them for some time.

Some females have two broods in a season, and there is often overlap in the care of the two families. For example, the ruby-throated hummingbird, one of the most northerly species, is known to have two or, depending on its location, three broods a

After a hasty foraging trip, a lone-parent female broad-billed hummingbird returns to the nest, top, and prepares to give her hatchling a billful of nectar and insects, above.

season. Where multiple broods occur, the industrious female starts building the next nest before the first clutch of chicks is gone.

Little Big Brain

It is difficult to measure animal intelligence. Yet unraveling the ways in which animals demonstrate thought, or what is known as cognition, occupies a great deal of research time for modern biologists. The reason is simple: Their findings can help answer questions about how a bird survives and reproduces.

The hummingbird is a particularly fascinating subject. Within the avian family, a tiny hummer understandably has the smallest bird brain of all, measuring roughly the size of a pea. Yet relative to body size, a hummingbird's brain is about 4.2 percent of its body weight, which is among the largest brain-to-body-weight ratios of all birds. By that same measure, hummingbirds put humans to shame. The human brain, while 7,000 times larger than that of a hummingbird, represents only 2 percent of our body weight, which makes the hummer's brain nearly twice as large by proportion.

Measuring a hummingbird's brain power is a tricky business. Scientists can't communicate directly with a wild species. To learn about a hummingbird's "thought" processes, researchers must investigate indirectly, by devising experiments that pose such questions as: How does a hum-

The territorial rufous hummingbird relies on memory to lead it back to a good food source.

mingbird locate its food sources? And, once it does, how is it able to return time and again to the same flower patch?

The answers are surprising. Tiny though it may be, the hummingbird's brain allows it to engage in complex behaviors. For centuries, common folklore has told us that hummingbirds simply prefer to feed at red flowers. While these birds do have an instinct to explore colorful objects, which explains why they are attracted to red, new research is showing that hungry hummers are much more than hardwired avian automatons irresistibly drawn to nature's crimson beacons. In fact, these birds employ sophisticated mental abilities, such as learning and memory, when locating food.

Hummingbirds possess innate navigational abilities that help them find their way. They can also remember the location of a flower patch and the contents of the blooms. When a flower rewards them with nectar, hummers are able to return to the feeding location with complete accuracy.

Experiments have shown that hummingbirds find the spot again regardless of surrounding landmarks, directional cues or the position of the flowers themselves. This enduring sense of space has been proved in several experiments in which scientists allowed hummingbirds to learn the location of nectar-rich flowers, then moved the flower patch a few feet from its original location. Even though the flower patch was still within sight of the hummers, the birds doggedly defended its original location. Scientists such as Canadian researcher Andrew Hurly of Alberta's University of Lethbridge, who has conducted many of these experiments, believe the birds carry the memory of position with them in the form of a "mental map" that provides a picture of im-

Although they don't have a preference for red flowers, hummingbirds are curious by nature and instinctively explore colorful objects.

portant features in the world around them.

To understand the role of color in helping hummingbirds find food, Hurly presented male rufous hummingbirds in the wild with arrays of two-tone artificial flowers, in all kinds of color combinations —white, blue, green, pink, red, orange, yellow and purple. Some of the flowers contained a sucrose solution. Once the birds learned the locations of the nectar-filled flowers, the researchers manipulated the position and color of individual flowers within each array.

The rufous hummingbirds made fewer errors in pinpointing a nectar reward when the flowers occupied the same position between arrays. They chose flowers based on their position even if the color was altered or the surrounding flowers were rearranged. Color, it turns out, plays a secondary role in helping hummingbirds remember and identify food sources. The birds could find the flowers faster when color cues were present. But Hurly believes that as long as spatial information is available, a color pattern has secondary significance in the hummingbirds' ability to locate a food source.

How could such an inflexible sense of space benefit a bird? The answer is simple: Patches of flowers in the wild don't normally uproot themselves and move, whereas colors come and go. Foraging according to position instead of color, therefore, is far more reliable. For high-performance hummingbirds, efficient feeding translates into greater success. When a hummingbird can locate a food source and then return to it without having to conduct an exhaustive search each time, it saves energy for important tasks, like defending a territory, building a nest and raising a family, and creates free time for resting.

Trip Takers

In the endless quest for a good supply of nectar, hummingbirds are often on the move. Some species make the rounds of flowers that come into bloom sequentially, while others, such as those living in the tropical highlands, move up and down the mountainside over the course of a day.

Several hummingbirds, however, make seasonal long-range trips known as migrations. With the exception of a few species, such as the Anna's and Allen's hummers, which stay primarily in their warm California range year-round, all North American hummingbird species migrate. Some of the most familiar temperate names—rufous, ruby-throated, calliope and black-chinned—venture thousands of miles north in the summer and then return to their overwintering grounds when the weather turns cold and nectar-filled flowers disappear.

Long-distance flight is a taxing proposition for the hummingbird. In its day-to-day life, it burns carbohydrates in order to hover, saving its fat stores to fuel bursts of power or for emergencies following times of prolonged fasting. For the long haul of migration, however, the hummingbird burns high-energy fat. Gram for gram, fat has a higher energy value than carbohydrates, which means more fuel (for better mileage) from less mass.

When it comes to fueling up for a long-distance flight, small size does have its ad-

A rubythroat, top, is among the widest-ranging members of the hummingbird family. Tropical cloud forest is home to dozens of species, center, while the rufous travels north to Alaska, bottom.

vantages. The smaller the bird, the faster it accumulates fat, so even a modest amount of weight gain makes a big difference to a hummingbird's energy stores. Scientists believe that a rubythroat carrying as little as 2.1 grams of fat should be able to fly more than 600 miles (960 km) nonstop. Such an increase in fat stores—more than 50 percent—helps explain how the diminutive rubythroat can fly over open water, across the Gulf of Mexico.

Competition, scientists believe, is the driving force behind hummingbird migration. Despite its risks and dangers, migration offers species the opportunity to relocate to less densely populated areas, which increases the chances for successfully raising offspring.

Not only do hummingbirds cover great distances, but they can locate their seasonal homes with pinpoint accuracy. One migratory rufous hummingbird was recaptured the following year at the original Canadian banding site. Many researchers have established that animals have an innate navigational sense, and hummingbirds possess the ability to return to locations as if they were using a compass.

Unlike geese or ducks, which migrate in flocks, hummingbirds fly solo. Instinct tells them to journey north. Sometimes when the birds arrive, the spring flowers have not yet opened. During these times, they survive by feeding on insects and at hummingbird feeders placed outside by homeowners.

On their return migration south, males of many species leave the breeding grounds first. They are followed by the females and then the juveniles. The trip south is less urgent than the flight north in spring. The birds follow a succession of flowering plants until they make the final leg of their journey to the tropics. One rufous hummingbird traveled some 750 miles (1,200 km) in 15 days and even gained weight during the trip.

All of the some 19 species of hummingbirds that regularly visit North America spend the winter in Mexico and Central America, while a handful of species—Costa's, black-chinned, Anna's, Allen's—overwinter in southern California and Arizona.

RECORD BREAKERS

The five greatest records for distance between banding and recovery points for hummingbirds are held by the rufous hummingbird. The longest trip was made by an adult female that traveled 1,732 miles (2,787 km). The second longest trip was also made by an adult female that traveled 1,373 miles (2,210 km), or about 33 miles (53 km) per day, from where she was banded on Vancouver Island to where she was recovered in New Mexico.

The smallest long-distance bird migrant in the world is the calliope hummingbird, which weighs under three grams ($\frac{1}{10}$ ounce) and travels nearly 2,000 miles (3,220 km) between its winter and summer homes.

The most northerly traveler is the rufous hummingbird, which migrates as far north as southern Alaska before returning to its winter home in Mexico, more than 2,000 miles (3,220 km) south.

Although the rufous hummingbird represents one of the most widely distributed hummingbird species, its traditional North American range was in the West. However, there have been an increasing number of eastern sightings, including reported appearances in all the midwestern and eastern United States plus most of the Canadian provinces east of Alberta.

Hummers by Nature

The study of the interactions between a hummingbird and its environment is the science of ecology. Biologists understand the word environment to mean all manner of relationships, from the effects that temperature and habitat have on the hummer to threats from predators and competitors.

Looking at these links reminds us that the hummingbird has a very sophisticated and intricate life. The close partnership between hummingbirds and flowers, for example, has been shaped by the thousands of years they have influenced one another, in what biologists call "coadaptation." Flowers which evolved to produce nectar then had a reward that attracted the birds and benefited the flowers, which were pollinated as the high-energy hummers moved from plant to plant.

While ecologists consider a variety of relationships in a species' life, such as its connections with its surroundings and with other species, they are also interested in the origin of behavior. Consider the hummingbird's nest, a tightly woven structure reinforced by superdurable spider silk and densely lined with plant down. It is easy to assume that the hummingbird's efficient nest is a direct response to its small size. In other words, being tiny makes it hard to keep warm; so the pint-sized female hummer constructs an insulated nest simply to keep herself and her two eggs warm during incubation. But what happens if we turn that theory on its head? Perhaps by developing its nest-building skills, the hummingbird of ancient times permitted the family to evolve into smaller birds. Scientists accept that many processes can occur and influence one another at the same time.

Questions about the connections in nature don't have cut-and-dried answers. The only way we can truly understand wild species is to embrace their complexity and consider them in the context of their environment in the broadest sense: where and how they live; where they've come from; and the alliances that exist among species. That analysis also includes the relationship between hummingbirds and humans.

Through the Ages

Few birds are as full of life and energy as is the hummingbird. Whether you spot one visiting a backyard feeder or defending a patch of exotic flowers in the tropical forest, you're witnessing one of nature's most amazing success stories.

Evolution tells us that birds share a common ancestry, despite the fact that they can vary widely in appearance. Examination of fossilized remains discovered in the 1860s has led scientists to believe that the species of birds which exist today started life on Earth with a reptilian ancestor some 150 million years ago. An interesting puzzle for biologists to ponder is how birds progressed from a lizardlike creature in the Jurassic period to the 10,000 species we see today.

The hummingbird family is an evolutionary superstar. With some 330 living species swelling its ranks, it is the second largest family of birds in the New World. Of the 110 genera in North and South America, more than half contain only a single species, and these occupy every available vegetation-rich niche. Such diversity and widespread distribution, or radiation of species, signal a remarkable evolutionary achievement.

The force that allows the genetic makeup of a population to change, or evolve, over time is called natural selection. Natural selection describes the mechanism that allows species to adapt characteristics, or traits, which make them fit to survive and thrive. Both physically and behaviorally, hummingbirds form one of the most unusual avian families, making them fascinating to study. What evolutionary path did they travel to

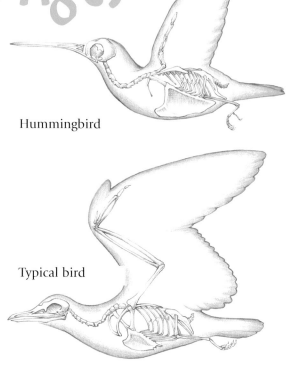

Hummingbird

Typical bird

The hummingbird has shorter arm bones and longer hand bones than most birds.

arrive at their present state? At what point in time did the changes occur that distinguish hummingbirds from all other bird species?

Scientists believe that the swift is the hummingbird's closest living relative. Skeletal similarities, like the proportions of the wing bones, are common to both families. Equally revealing, however, are behaviors such as comparable nesting styles, the number of white eggs each lays and the dependency of their young. Both families also conserve energy by becoming "torpid" when faced with cold weather or food shortages.

DNA studies, however, show that the relationship is actually a distant one. It is estimated that the two families began to diverge from a common ancestor about 59 million years ago. It took another 40 million years before the hummingbird ancestor of today's hermit and non-hermit subfamilies appeared. The older hermit group, which remains much smaller, less diversified and less colorful, may have served as the foundation that later gave rise to non-hermit species.

Robert Bleiweiss of the University of Wisconsin has used DNA testing to establish the chronological appearance of six non-hermit hummingbird groups. They are roughly divided into mangoes (lowland species); brilliants (a group of species evolved from a shared ancestor and living in the South American Andes); coquettes (a mountain-dwelling group of species); emeralds (typically iridescent-green species); mountain-gems (large-bodied species); and the Cuban bee hummingbird (the diminutive species in the family).

How and why did hummingbirds appear? Scientists believe that a number of factors were involved. Geologic change, such as the upheaval of the Andes Mountains in South America, where nearly half of all species are found, created new habitats that a specialized bird family might exploit. Climate change and a diversification of flowering plants that began to dominate the landscape may also have played a role. From its original equatorial home, the family spread northward, ending with the emergence of North American species some six million years ago.

Factors beyond global geological events can also drive evolution. The changes within the family were ongoing as species diverged into a variety of specialized hummingbird types that coevolved with flowers. Research by a biologist working on St. Lucia has provided the first evidence connecting ecological factors (such as various feeding opportunities) to evolutionary differences. For many years, scientists have known that the bill of the female purple-throated carib is nearly one-third longer than that of the male. But only recently have they found that each sex feeds at a differently shaped flower, which closely matches the particular shape of its bill. They speculate that this adaptation evolved to allow the competing sexes to divvy up available food sources.

The swift is believed to be the closest living relative of the hummingbird family.

Naturalist Charles Darwin's early-19th-century discovery of 14 finches, the most diversified family of animals he found on the isolated Galápagos Islands, was a telling starting point for developing his theory of evolution. But it pales in comparison with the diversity of hummingbirds. Each time you look at a hummingbird, you're seeing millions of years of avian history, the product of a never-ending process that shapes and transforms populations by pressures and forces of survival.

Partners From Paradise

Hummingbirds have an ancient and close relationship with flowers. Like two friends who have grown up together, hummingbirds and the flowers at which they feed have adapted together, bill-in-blossom, since each came into existence.

The relationship between hummingbirds and flowers is mutually beneficial, which simply means that each gets something positive from the other. While all hummingbird species enjoy eating insects, most spend their days foraging for the sugary-sweet nectar produced by flowers. Rich in calories and easy to metabolize, nectar is a high-octane staple in their diet.

In return for feeding their hummingbird visitors, flowers benefit by recruiting one of the most hardworking and reliable of nature's pollinating forces. For a great majority of the world's plants, pollination is the first step in reproduction. Pollen must be transported from the male parts of one flower to the female parts of another of the same species. Most microscopic pollen of flowering plants is too heavy to blow on the wind, and it is up to animals and insects to transport it. As a warm-blooded animal, the hummingbird has a competitive advantage over insects because, unlike weather-sensitive bees and flies, the hummer covers its daily routes come rain or shine, feeding on the run, even as it ascends into mountainous tropical forests. And each time it hovers in front of a blossom to drink the nectar, the hummingbird is dusted with pollen, which it then carries to its next feeding stop at a neighboring plant.

There is little doubt that the compatibility between hummers and their flowers evolved in concert over thousands of years. Biologists estimate that more than 150 flowering plant species in North America alone have changed or modified their shape, size, color and nectar content to attract foraging hummingbirds. Like most birds, but unlike insects, hummingbirds can see in color, and

Hummingbirds, like the emerald-bellied puffleg, opposite, and the copper-rumped, below, are reliable pollinators. Feeding in all kinds of weather, they pick up and transfer pollen between flowers.

as a result, many of the flowers they visit and pollinate are red. Similarly, researchers have found that many hummingbird-pollinated plants have no fragrance and offer no "landing pad" to entice visiting insects. Nectar itself serves no functional purpose for flowers other than to attract hungry pollinators. The prolonged blooming season of many hummingbird-dependent flowers appears to be an ecological tip-of-the-hat to the hummingbird's year-round activity.

Many of the physical adaptations of hummingbirds have strengthened their relationships with particular flower species. Long saberlike bills and grooved tongues are obvious examples of a morphology specially adapted to feed on reservoirs of nectar hidden deep inside the base of a

Its downcurved bill makes the long-tailed hermit a good match for the heliconia.

flower. In addition, the hummers' mode of hovering flight allows them to extract the nectar noninvasively, with a gentle "kiss."

Among a handful of hummingbird species, however, there are more striking instances of adaptation that illustrate the coevolution of hummingbirds and flowers. In the rainforest of Costa Rica, for example, heliconia flowers, members of the banana family, are pollinated by hermit hummingbirds. The deep flowers are a perfect fit for the hermit's gently downcurved bill, while the heliconia's unwelcoming spearlike red flowers exclude generalist pollinators such as bees and flies.

Some hummingbird-flower relationships

Unable to reach the nectar with its short bill, the stripe-tailed hummingbird pierces the base of the flower's corolla to feed from the bottom.

are so exclusive that the shape, depth and length of the blossom is precisely designed by natural selection to match the contours of a specific hummingbird's bill. One such example is the Andean sword-billed hummingbird, whose bill ranges from three to four inches (83-105 mm) in length. Only the swordbill can feed from the 4½-inch-deep (114 mm) corolla of the passion-flower, which is virtually inaccessible to other species that sport shorter bills.

The tried-and-true relationship between hummingbirds and flowers has evolved over millennia. It is, at once, mutually beneficial and sometimes necessary for survival.

Ticket to Ride

Another organism that benefits from the relationship between hummingbirds and flowers is a mite. Native to the tropical New World, the flower-dwelling mites rely on visiting hummingbirds to transport them from one plant to another.

The mite runs up the feeding hummer's bill and waits in the bird's nasal cavity until it "smells" the new flower, which is the eyeless mite's sensory cue that the "hummingbird express" has pulled in at its preferred blossom. Though the mite is smaller than a pinhead, it zooms the length of the hummingbird's bill in less than five seconds.

The Family Tree

Distinctive and dazzling, the hummingbird presented an unusual problem for the early naturalists who wanted to study it. The combination of the small bird's high-speed lifestyle, darting flight and widespread distribution through sometimes remote areas made the identification and classification of members of the hummingbird family a challenge.

From Christopher Columbus on, explorers were captivated by hummingbirds, but the first scientific description of them didn't appear until 1671 in Great Britain. And in the tenth edition of *Systema Natura*, published in 1758, Swedish botanist Carolus Linnaeus —whose lifelong work classifying plant and animal species has become the foundation of modern taxonomy—named just 18 hummingbird species, a mere 3 percent of the entire family. (Detail-oriented though Linnaeus may have been by nature, he was not perfect. Of the 18 species he named, only 11, in fact, were distinct.) A flurry of naturalist activity soon followed, and by the 1850s, records existed for nearly half the total number of currently recognized hummingbird species. But it was not until the mid-1900s that the list was considered complete.

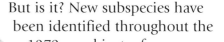

Eighteenth-century Swedish botanist and classification expert Carolus Linnaeus recorded early descriptions of hummingbird species.

But is it? New subspecies have been identified throughout the 1970s, and just a few years ago, scientists working in the mountains of southeast Colombia discovered a previously unknown hummingbird, different in body form, habits and habitat. They labeled it the west Andean emerald.

While hummingbirds are found only in the New World, their hemispheric isolation has not limited their success. In fact, hummingbirds have made excellent use of the available terrain. The some 330 species of these tiny birds are spread out between Alaska in the north and Tierra del Fuego in the south. In South America, they reach their western boundary at Juan Fernández, a group of islands some 400 miles (645 km) off the coast of Chile, and their eastern boundary at Joâo Pessoa in Brazil. Individual hummingbird species have learned to exploit a variety of habitats, including offshore islands, lush lowland forests, coastal mangrove swamps, deserts, subarctic meadows, temperate forests, interior plains and Andean glaciers located some 15,000 feet (4,575 m) above sea level.

Scientists believe that the hummingbird family's widespread distribution, or radiation, began in its ancestral home somewhere in South America. Even today, the greatest concentration of species occurs within a 10-degree band straddling the equator, and the numbers decrease with altitude above sea level and distance from the equator. Ecuador boasts the greatest number of species, at 163, followed by Colombia, with 135. Costa Rica has 52 species, and given that country's tiny size, this represents the densest concentration of species. North of Mexico, the numbers drop off dramatically: 19 species call the United States home, while only 5 species regularly visit Canada each year.

Competition is a deciding factor in

The broad-billed hummingbird lives primarily in Mexico but is a migratory species throughout southern Arizona and southwestern New Mexico and Texas.

determining where hummingbirds range and how they behave. It's in the best interest of each species to avoid too much overlapping of ranges and habitats. In North America, hummingbirds exhibit what biologists call ecological segregation. Over time, the birds have come to occupy distinctive habitats where they experience less competition. For example, the five species that spend the summer in Canada embark on their massive migrations solely for the breeding season, and in their wide-open northern spaces, they are the only species in the area.

In the tropics, on the other hand, different species can be densely clustered. To succeed without unnecessary competition, hummingbird species form "guilds," which can include dozens of species. Because each species specializes in its favorite habitat, foraging method and flowers, an uneasy peace exists within the guild. Territorial residents avoid the wandering trapliners, which in turn have little to do with transient migrants. In Mexico's interior highlands, scientists discovered that the berylline hummer, which is a bright bronzy metallic-green color, moved at altitudes between 3,000 and 9,850 feet (900-3,000 m), surviving on flowers amid pine, oak and fir at the forest edge. Within the same area, the blue-throated hummingbird worked at altitudes between 5,900 and 9,850 feet (1,800-3,000 m). While there was some overlap at the highest altitudes, the competition naturally became diffused because the blue-throated hummer preferred mountain meadows.

Hazards for Hummers

Hummingbirds fascinated New World indigenous peoples for centuries. They similarly captivated European settlers, who quickly realized that the brilliantly colored little birds were worth their weight in gold. Like the snowy egret and the peacock, which were valued for their elaborate plumage, hummingbirds became a hot commodity with design houses in the 17th century. Hundreds of thousands of hummingbird skins were shipped to Europe for all manner of uses in the decorative arts, from still-life arrangements to hat adornments.

After centuries of exploitation, hummingbirds were formally protected under the Migratory Bird Treaty Act of 1918. The act prohibited killing birds that migrated between Canada and the United States and outlawed buying, selling and possessing their parts, such as feathers, and their nests. By the 1970s, this protection extended into Mexico, and by 1987, the conservation movement had raised our awareness of the vulnerability of wildlife species, resulting in the Convention on International Trade in Endangered Species (CITES), which explicitly protects all hummingbird species. Today, it is estimated that some 27 hummingbird species are threatened, another 22 species are near threatened, 7 are endangered, and 12 are vulnerable.

While humans are now consciously trying to protect hummingbirds, human actions indirectly continue to create problems. The hummingbird family itself is diverse, but many of its species have evolved into specialists that live in isolated or specific areas and therefore have specialized needs. The destruction of forests to create farmland in Central and South America robs hummingbirds of precious habitat. In North America, the clearing of rural countryside to accommodate urban sprawl eliminates many of the hummingbirds' favorite plants. For example, as many as 17 species of resident and migrant hummingbirds in southern Arizona travel what are known as nectar corridors—flowers in bloom that run from the southern states into Mexico. These areas are among the fastest-vanishing habitats in the state, and their fragmentation can threaten the survival of birds that rely on the continuous feeding sites.

Pesticides, used to control the spread of weeds and insects, pose an ongoing threat to hummingbirds. Pesticides can accumulate in the environment in a process scientists call biomagnification, in which relatively dilute applications become amplified with each step up the food chain. Since hummers feed on insects, they ingest high concentrations of harmful chemicals.

Where human housing and buildings

Many hummingbird species, like Costa Rica's magenta-throated woodstar, are vulnerable to destruction of habitat due to development.

In hummingbird-rich Costa Rica, home to 52 species, clearing forests for farmland, left, and clear-cutting, right, destroy vital habitat.

occur, the single most important cause of mortality among hummingbirds in the United States is flying full speed into a closed window. Red electric-fence insulators once represented another danger to hummers, and in the mid-1980s, the National Audubon Society called for a ban on their manufacture. Several reports over a two-year period showed that the bright color attracted foraging birds which were then electrocuted when probing an opening in the insulator in search of food.

Severe weather is the most serious natural hazard hummingbirds face. Frost or prolonged cold and wet can be perilous, as the small birds are unable to keep themselves warm enough. Conversely, extremely dry periods cause flowers to wither, depriving hummers of a much-needed food source. And while few bird species are known as hummingbird hunters, a 1978 scientific record suggests that the tiny hawk may spe-

cialize in capturing hummingbirds. Attacks on hummingbirds by frogs, snakes, insects, fish and mammals have also been reported.

A more likely source of calamity for the diminutive hummer, however, is becoming entangled in a spiderweb. Many tropical webs are larger and stronger than the hummer itself. The golden orb weaver, for instance, spins a three-foot-wide (1 m) web across forest trails and through the understory. When a hummingbird tries to hijack an insect from a spiderweb or grab some silk to reinforce its nest, it runs the risk of becoming trapped. At La Selva Biological Research Station in Costa Rica, one scientist witnessed several such incidents when hummers were caught in the sticky silk, fell to the ground and then became coated in leaf debris and twigs. Unable to free themselves, the birds died of exhaustion or were captured by predators.

With the support of humans who hang feeders, create gardens, plant new trees for cover and, most important, tread lightly on Earth, hummingbirds will have a far greater chance of survival.

Hummingbird Havens

One of the best ways to see and study hummingbirds is to "invite" them to visit your yard. Curious by nature, hummingbirds will readily explore feeders, and while there is a range of feeders available that will attract the birds, you don't need to spend a lot of money to be successful. Look for a feeder that has prominent red feeding stations—bell- or trumpet-shaped—and is easy to clean.

If pizza rules your life, you'll easily understand that hummingbirds prefer one food above all others: sugary water. You can prepare their favorite drink by mixing one part sugar in four parts water. Begin by boiling the water, and stir in the sugar while the water is still hot. Refrigerate the solution until it has completely cooled, then fill the feeder. The remaining "nectar" can be stored in the refrigerator for up to two weeks. It is important that you use only white sugar and never mix the nectar with sugar substitutes, such as syrup or honey, which can give the birds a fatal fungal infection. Food dyes are similarly dangerous to hummingbirds and must not be added to the nectar.

You can increase the chances of attracting hummingbirds by placing several feeders near each other. Choose a spot that is out of bright sunlight but still in plain view. If ants become interested in the feeder, grease the cord it hangs from with petroleum jelly or cooking oil to discourage access. Or experiment with a baffler using a plastic plate partially filled with water and mounted above the feeder, where it works like a moat to block the insects' paths.

While you don't need to buy an elaborate feeder, it is important to be diligent in maintaining the one you do choose. Hummingbird feeders must be cleaned and washed on a regular basis to discourage the growth of deadly bacteria. Once a week, empty and clean the feeder with either a 10 percent bleach solution or vinegar, and scour with a bottle brush. If you have trouble dislodging dirt, allow the feeder to soak briefly in hot water. Then, most important of all, rinse the container with hot water, followed by cold water, making sure all traces of cleanser are removed. (In general, experts advise against using soap to wash the feeder because the birds do not like the residue left behind by detergents.)

A broad-tailed hummingbird and a praying mantis time-share a feeder, a simple device that will attract hummers to your yard.

ers will catch a hummer's attention, and I have witnessed ruby-throated hummingbirds investigating a variety of colorful potted plants, such as impatiens and nasturtium. Wildflowers likewise offer a rich nectar supply, and your local garden nursery can recommend a variety of blooms. With their long, probing bills, hummingbirds are well suited to tubular or bell-shaped blossoms, like lobelia, bee balm, hollyhock, lily, trumpet vine and salvia, and stands of single-species patches work best to draw hummers to your garden.

It's important that your hummingbird garden is a pesticide-free zone. Wildflower species native to your area will already be hardened to withstand climate fluctuations. If the soil is healthy and fortified with organic compost, your flowers will resist most pest infestations. Any pest solutions should be organic, or you'll risk harming the birds you are working hard to attract.

Hummingbirds are entertaining to watch. Once a few start visiting your yard, you can sit back and enjoy hours of at-home nature study. ⅄

Hollyhocks with multiple trumpet-shaped flowers, above, attract hummingbirds and are a natural food source to complement feeders, below.

Once the feeder is clean, refill it with fresh nectar.

Your interest in flowers and gardening will also encourage hummingbirds to visit your yard. Not only do hummingbird-friendly gardens offer you an insider's look at fascinating hummingbird behaviors, such as feeding and defending food sources, but by planting these flowers, you're helping increase hummingbird habitat, which is essential for their survival.

A number of flow-

Hummers & Humans

Only after explorers came to the New World in the 15th century were hummingbirds first studied and described in scientific journals. Long before Europeans arrived in what would later be called North and South America, however, these engaging species had been known to indigenous people for thousands of years. Like other animals with great symbolic power—the wolf, grizzly, eagle, raven and coyote, to name a few—the hummingbird was etched into the beliefs, art and artifacts of pre-Columbian cultures.

Aboriginal people celebrated the hummingbird's powers. Its fairylike presence and the changeability of its appearance—dazzling in sunlight and subdued in shadow—added to its mystique and made the hummingbird the focal point of many spiritual legends in the Aztec, Mayan and Nazca cultures.

In one Mayan legend, for example, the hummingbird is the last avian creation,

Etched on a Peruvian plateau by Nazca people some 1,500 years ago, a 300-foot (90 m) hummingbird silhouette reflects the bird's symbolic importance in human spirituality and beliefs.

cobbled together from spare parts of other birds but endowed with the power to hover at and feed from flowers. When the original male and female hummers chose to marry, the story goes on, other bird species took pity on these avian "leftovers" and shared some of their own finest attire with them. The brilliant South American quetzal imparted iridescent-green feathers, the house finch added a red gorget, and the swallow handed down its striking white-feather highlights.

In other legends, the hummingbird is the sun in disguise, and a Mohave tale mentions a tiny bird leading people from the underground into the bright surface world. The Taino people of Florida and the Caribbean told Columbus that the hummer was once a common fly. Its powers of transformation originated perhaps because, as a pollinator, it is identified as a life-giving symbol. To this day, throughout Central and South America, the hummingbird's influence earns its image a place on good-luck charms and love amulets.

To celebrate its magical powers, native artists used representations of the hummingbird in tapestries, ceramics and architecture. Its feathers adorned ceremonial garments, and the word hummingbird itself pervades the ancient languages. As a symbol of submission, Montezuma gave Hernando Cortés a headdress adorned with hundreds of hummingbird skins. For its sheer scale, the most impressive representation of a hummingbird is a stark 300-foot (90 m) silhouette etched on a Peruvian plateau by Nazca people some 1,500 years ago.

Spanish explorers in the late 16th century found images of Huitzilopochtli—the Aztec war god and the most celebrated of

PLATE 15

TROCHILUS ORNATUS, Male.
(The Tufted necked Humming-Bird.)

Europeans marveled at the elaborate plumage of the New World's hummingbirds and illustrated many species in painstaking detail.

Mexican deities—being transformed into a hummingbird. The names of many Aztec gods were influenced by the hummingbird: Huitzilopochtli ("hummingbird on the left," or "hummingbird to the south"); Huitzilihuite ("hummingbird feather"); and Xochiquetzal ("flower bird"). Among the Taino, the bravest warriors were labeled *colibri*, a term that has been translated into several European languages as the common word for hummingbird.

Throughout history, the tiny bird with burnished wings has been a source of inspiration, a symbol of life and a touchstone for our vision of tropical paradise.

Hummers On-line

The virtual world of the Internet offers nature lovers a bird's-eye view of hummingbirds. With its interactive programming, the World Wide Web is a dynamic partner for keeping you up to date and involved in the emerging knowledge of one of nature's most engaging species.

www.portalproductions.com/

The Hummingbird Web Site is an excellent source of information on all aspects of the tiny birds' lives. Straightforward categories let you research everything on North American species, from plumage and nests to migration. This site is loaded with lots of fascinating trivia and photographs.

www.hummingbirds.net

Operated out of St. Louis, Missouri, this is one of the Internet's more comprehensive hummingbird sites. Pull-down menus list a wide range of topics for users to browse. Each category is full of information on attracting, watching, feeding and studying hummingbirds, plus there's a calendar of events for hummingbird festivals around the United States and a useful question-and-answer department. The site also boasts some nifty innovations, such as a hummingbird "mouse trail" that tracks your cursor as it scans the page, recorded hummingbird calls and a handful of QuickTime movie clips of rubythroats in action at a feeder. (Watch for the male's darting tongue as he approaches the nectar source.) Take your time to search through the library of still pictures in the on-line gallery.

www.rubythroat.org/DetailsMain.html

If conservation is of special interest to you, check out Operation RubyThroat: The Hummingbird Project. This site is the focal point for an international, interdisciplinary education-and-research initiative at Hilton Pond Center for Piedmont Natural History in York, South Carolina. Designed for students in Central and North America, including Belize, Canada, Costa Rica, El Salvador, Guatemala, Honduras, Mexico, Nicaragua, Panama and the United States, the site invites visitors to make observations and post data and keeps the world up to date on late-breaking rubythroat research.

www.learner.org/jnorth/tm/humm/About.html

Journey North, a well-respected interactive site devoted to the global study of wildlife travels, has a hummingbird-migration study under way. If you're a dedicated backyard birder, check out its call for reports of hummingbird activities. You don't have to be a trained biologist to participate. The survey draws heavily on amateur naturalists' contributions to increase our understanding of the birds' movements. Such ordinary details as when your feeder goes up and the arrival and departure dates of your first and last hummingbird visitors can help fill in the information gap in scientists' understanding of the delightful hummer. This site also has fun facts and many excellent links to useful hummingbird trivia.

Photo Credits

3: © Tim Fitzharris

5: © Robert McCaw

6: © John R. Hicks/DRK Photo

8: © Fulvio Eccardi/Bruce Coleman Inc.

10: © Sid and Shirley Rucker/DRK Photo

11: Both photos © Sid and Shirley Rucker/DRK Photo

12: © Bob and Clara Calhoun/Bruce Coleman Inc.

13: © Tim Fitzharris

14: Top photo © Kenneth W. Fink/Bruce Coleman Inc.

14: Bottom photo © Luis Mazariegos

15: Both photos © Michael and Patricia Fogden

16: Left photo © Turid Forsyth

16: Right photo © Michael Fogden/Earth Scenes

17: © Luis Mazariegos

18: © Michael and Patricia Fogden

19: © Luis Mazariegos

20: © Stephen Dalton/Animals Animals

21: Top photo © Stephen J. Krasemann/DRK Photo

21: Bottom photo © Michael and Patricia Fogden

22: © Michael and Patricia Fogden

24: © Michael and Patricia Fogden

25: © Sid and Shirley Rucker/DRK Photo

26: © Michael and Patricia Fogden

27: © Michael and Patricia Fogden

28: © Michael and Patricia Fogden

29: Top photo © Michael and Patricia Fogden

29: Bottom photo © Wayne Lankinen/DRK Photo

30: © Art Wolfe Inc.

31: Top photo © Stephen J. Krasemann/DRK Photo

31: Bottom photo © Alan G. Nelson/Animals Animals

32: Left photo © John Cancalosi/DRK Photo

32: Right photo © Michael and Patricia Fogden

33: © Stephen J. Krasemann/DRK Photo

34: © Stephen Dalton/Animals Animals

35: Top photo © Sid and Shirley Rucker/DRK Photo

35: Bottom photo © Michael and Patricia Fogden

36: © Jeff Foott/DRK Photo

37: © Michael and Patricia Fogden

38: © Robert Lubeck/Animals Animals

39: Both photos © Sid and Shirley Rucker/DRK Photo

40: © Tim Fitzharris

41: © C.C. Lockwood/DRK Photo

42: Top photo © C.C. Lockwood/Animals Animals

42: Middle photo © Turid Forsyth

42: Bottom photo © Eastcott/Momatiuk/Earth Scenes

44: © Barbara Gerlach/DRK Photo

46: Both illustrations by Marta Scythes

47: © Alan G. Nelson/Animals Animals

48: © Luis Mazariegos

49: © Maresa Pryor/Animals Animals

50: © C. Farnetti/Animals Animals

51: © Michael and Patricia Fogden

52: from *Natural History of Humming Birds*, Vol. 1 (Edinburgh, 1834)

53: © Wayne Lankinen/DRK Photo

54: © Michael Fogden/DRK Photo

55: Both photos © Turid Forsyth

56: © Sid and Shirley Rucker/ DRK Photo

57: Top photo © Turid Forsyth

57: Bottom photo © Robert McCaw

58: © Charles and Josette Lenars/CORBIS

59: Illustration by Pennant, from *Natural History of Humming Birds*, Vol. 1 (Edinburgh, 1834)

61: Steely-vented hummingbird © Michael and Patricia Fogden

Green violet-ear hummingbird icon throughout *Hummingbirds: A Beginner's Guide* © Michael and Patricia Fogden

Index

Aboriginal myths about hummingbirds, 58-59

Adaptations of hummingbirds to particular flowers, 50

Albumen, 34

Allen's hummingbird, 30, 42, 43

Altricial chicks, 36

Amethyst woodstar hummingbird, 29

Andean hillstar hummingbird, 11, 34, 39

Anna's hummingbird, 13, 26, 30, 32, 36, 38, 42, 43; photos, 25, 32

Appetite, 24

Attracting hummingbirds to a backyard, 56-57

Audubon, John James, 18

Band-tailed barbthroat hummingbird, 38

Barbs, 18

Barbthroat hummingbird, band-tailed, 38

Bat, bumblebee, 12

Bearded helmetcrest hummingbird, 11; photo, 14

Bee balm, 57

Bee hummingbird, Cuban, 9, 12, 47

Behavior, 23-43

Berylline hummingbird, 14, 31, 53

Bills
and flower type, 15, 51
length and shape, 14-15

Biomagnification, 54

Black-chinned hummingbird, 32, 42, 43; photos, 33, 35

Black-crested coquette hummingbird, 27

Bleiweiss, Robert, 47

Blue-throated hummingbird, 12, 31, 53; photo, 12

Bones. See Skeleton

Brain, 40, 41

Brilliant hummingbirds, 47
green-crowned, photo, 21

Broad-billed hummingbird, photos, 10, 39, 53

Broad-tailed hummingbird, photos, 13, 36, 56

Brood patch, 34

Buff-bellied hummingbird, 14

Calcium carbonate, 34

Calliope hummingbird, 30, 33, 42, 43; photo, 31

Camouflage of nests, 33

Candlestick flower, 23

Carib hummingbird, purple-throated, 47

Cheetahs, 11

Chicks
development, 39
feeding, 36-39
hatching, 36
protection from predators, 39

CITES (Convention on International Trade in Endangered Species), 45

Classification, scientific, of hummingbirds, 46-47, 52

Coadaptation, 45

Color
of hummingbird feathers, 18-20
perception, 17
role in food location, 41, 49-50
structural, 18

Coloration, interference, 20

Competition
and hummingbirds' range, 53
and migration, 43

Cone cells, 17

Convention on International Trade in Endangered Species, 45

Copper-rumped hummingbird, photo, 49

Coquette hummingbirds, 47
black-crested, 27
tufted, photo, 30

Costa's hummingbird, 30, 43

Courtship
displays, 30-31
leks, 31

Crowned woodnymph hummingbird, photo, 35

Dangers to hummingbirds, 54-55

Darwin, Charles, 47

Diet, 13, 24-25. See also Food

Displays, courtship, 30-31

Distances traveled by hummingbirds, 43

Ecological segregation, 53

Ecology of hummingbirds, 45-59

Egg tooth, 35

Eggs, 34, 39
comparative sizes, photo, 34

Emerald hummingbirds, 25, 47
west Andean, 52

Emerald-bellied puffleg hummingbird, photo, 48

Energy
conservation of, 12-13, 45
for muscles, 11
need for, 12-13
need for when migrating, 42-43

Evolution of hummingbirds, 46-47

Exploitation of hummingbirds in the past, 54

Eyes, 16-17

Fat, body, 13
and energy needs for migration, 42-43

Feathers, 18-21
density in hummingbirds, 18
iridescence, 18-20
maintenance, 21
use in communication, 20-21
use to produce sounds, 20, 31

Feeders for hummingbirds, 56-57; 56, 57

Feeding
  chicks, 36-39
  method, 15
  strategies, 25-27
Feet, 11
Female, parental care
  given by, 36
Filchers, 27
Flamingos, 14
Flight, 28-29. See also
  Hovering flight
  courtship displays,
    30-31
  long-distance, 42-43
  maneuverability in, 28,
    29
  muscles, 11, 28-29
  shuttle, 30
Flowers
  adaptations to hum-
    mingbirds, 50-51
  attractive to humming-
    birds, 50, 57
  pollination strategies,
    26, 49
  relationship with hum-
    mingbirds, 26, 45,
    49, 51
  type and bill length
    and shape, 15
Food, 13, 24-25. See also
  Feeding; Foraging
  strategies
  amount consumed by
    hummingbirds, 9
  locating, 40-41, 49-50
Foraging strategies, 25-27
Fovea centralis, 17
Giant hummingbird, 9, 34

Gleaning method of
  capturing insects, 25
Gorget, 17, 21
Green-crowned brilliant
  hummingbird, photo, 21
Green-fronted lancebill
  hummingbird, photo, 14
Green hermit humming-
  bird, 31
Guilds, 53
Habitat destruction, 54;
  photos, 55
Hatching, 35, 36
Hawking method of
  capturing insects, 16, 25
Heart, 12
Heart rate, 9, 12
Heat. See also Energy
  conservation of, 12, 45
  hummingbirds' need
    for, 12-13
Heliconia, 26, 50; photos,
  27, 50
Helmetcrest humming-
  bird, bearded, 11; photo,
  14
Hermit hummingbirds,
  18, 25, 26, 27, 47, 50
  green, 31
  little, 31
  long-tailed, 31, 33;
    photos, 27, 50
  straight-billed, photo,
  32
Hillstar hummingbirds, 34
  Andean, 11, 39
Hollyhocks, 57; photo, 57
Hovering flight, 10, 11, 29.
  See also Flight

Human dangers to hum-
  mingbirds, 54-55
Hurly, Andrew, 41
Impatiens, 57
Incubation, 34-35, 36
Insects in hummingbird
  diet, 25
Intelligence, 40-41
Interference coloration, 20
Iridescence of feathers, 18-
  20
Keratin, 14, 18
Lancebill hummingbird,
  green-fronted, photo, 14
Learning ability, 40
Leg band, photo, 11
Leks, 31
Lift, 28
Lilies, 57
Linnaeus, Carolus, *Systema
  Natura*, 52
Little hermit humming-
  bird, 31
Lobelia, 26, 57
Long-tailed hermit hum-
  mingbird, 31, 33;
  photos, 27, 50
Long-tailed sylph hum-
  mingbird, photo, 19
Magenta-throated wood-
  star hummingbird, 27;
  photos, 24, 54
Magnificent humming-
  bird, photos, 10, 11
Maneuverability in flight,
  28, 29
Mango hummingbirds, 47
Marauders, 27
Maternal care of eggs and
  chicks, 36-39

Mating, 31
Memory, 40
Metabolic rate, 12-13
Migrant hummingbirds,
  transient, 53
Migrations, 42-43
Migratory Bird Treaty Act,
  54
Mites, relationship with
  hummingbirds, 51
Mitochondria, 11
Molting, 21
Monarda, photo, 16
Mountain-gem humming-
  birds, 47
    purple-throated, 27;
    photo, 26
Muscles, 10-11
  flight, 11, 28-29
Mythology about hum-
  mingbirds, 58-59
Nasturtiums, 57
Native myths about hum-
  mingbirds, 58-59
Natural selection, 46
Navigational abilities,
  40-41
Nectar, 13, 24-25, 49
Nesting. See Incubation;
  Nests; Parental care
Nestlings. See Chicks
Nests, 32-33, 45
Nictitating membrane, 17
On-line hummingbird
  information, 60
Orb weaver spider, golden,
  55
Ostriches, 34
Parental care, 36-39
Passionflowers, 15, 51

Perching, 11

Pesticides and hummingbirds, 54, 57

Physical characteristics, 9-21

Platelets of feathers, 20

Plumage, 18-21. See also Feathers

Pollination strategies of flowers, 26, 49

Predators, 55
   protection of chicks from, 39

Puffleg hummingbirds, 25
   emerald-bellied, photo, 48

Purple-backed thornbill, 14

Purple-throated carib hummingbird, 47

Purple-throated mountain-gem hummingbird, 27; photo, 26

Quill, 18

Rachis, 18

Range, 52-53

Red, 17, 50

Relationship with flowers, 26, 45, 49-51

Retina, 17

Rod cells, 17

Ruby-throated hummingbird, 18, 25, 30, 31, 32-33, 38, 39, 42, 43, 57; photos, 6, 31, 42

Rufous hummingbird, 20, 23, 26, 30, 32, 38, 41, 42, 43; photos, 21, 29, 40, 42, 44

Rufous-tailed hummingbird, photo, 38

Sabrewing hummingbird, violet, photo, 15

Salvia, 57

Sap, 24

Sapsuckers, 24

Scientific description of hummingbirds, 52

Scintillant hummingbird, photos, 22, 28

Selection, natural, 46

Shrew, Etruscan, 12

Shuttle flights, 30

Sicklebill hummingbirds, 26
   white-tipped, photo, 15

Size, 9, 10

Skeleton, 10; illustration, 46
   and flight, 29

Snowcap hummingbird, photo, 29

Sounds made by feathers, 20, 31

Spider, golden orb weaver, 55

Spider silk in nests, 33

Spiderwebs as danger to hummingbirds, 55

Spoonbills, 14

Straight-billed hermit hummingbird, photo, 32

Stripe-tailed hummingbird, photos, 37, 51

Sugary water solution for feeding hummingbirds, 56

Sunangel hummingbirds, 25

Swifts, relationship to hummingbirds 46-47; photo, 47

Sword-billed hummingbird, 14, 15
   Andean, 51

Sylph hummingbirds, long-tailed, photo, 19

Systema Natura, by Carolus Linnaeus, 52

Temperature, body, 9, 12. See also Heat

Territorial hummingbirds, feeding strategy, 25-26, 53

Territory
   defense of, 26
   size, 25-26

Thornbill hummingbirds, 11
   purple-backed, 14

Thrushes, 18

Tongue, 15

Torpor, 9, 12-13

Traplining hummingbirds, feeding strategy, 25, 26-27, 53

Trumpet vine, 57

Tufted coquette hummingbird, photo, 30

Uniqueness of hummingbirds, 9

Violet-crowned hummingbird, 14

Violet-ear hummingbirds, 38
   white-vented, photo, 17

Violet-headed hummingbird, photo, 18

Violet sabrewing hummingbird, photo, 15

Vision, 16-17

Weather as danger to hummingbirds, 54

Websites with hummingbird information, 60

Weight, 10

West Andean emerald hummingbird, 52

White-eared hummingbird, 14, 31, 33

White-tipped sicklebill hummingbird, photo, 15

White-vented violet-ear hummingbird, photo, 17

Wine-throated hummingbird, photo, 8

Wings, 9. See also Flight, muscles
   bones, 10; illustration, 46
   length, 29
   movements in flight, 28, 29
   speed of beating, 9, 29

Woodnymph hummingbird, crowned, photo, 35

Woodpeckers, 24

Woodstar hummingbirds, amethyst, 29
   magenta-throated, 27; photos, 24, 54

Yolk, 34

Young. See Chicks